50 Dutch Oven Camping Dessert Recipes for Home

By: Kelly Johnson

Table of Contents

- Dutch Oven Apple Crisp
- Campfire Peach Cobbler
- Chocolate Lava Cake
- Camp Dutch Oven Brownies
- Pineapple Upside-Down Cake
- Dutch Oven Banana Bread
- Campfire S'mores Dip
- Blueberry Lemon Dump Cake
- Dutch Oven Cherry Clafoutis
- Cinnamon Roll Campfire Bake
- Dutch Oven Strawberry Shortcake
- Camp Dutch Oven Pineapple Cake
- Blackberry Cobbler
- Dutch Oven Pecan Pie
- Campfire Monkey Bread
- Dutch Oven Bread Pudding
- Orange Campfire Cake
- Dutch Oven Berry Crumble
- Campfire Peach Melba
- Dutch Oven Pumpkin Pie
- Camp Dutch Oven Apple Fritters
- Campfire Nutella S'mores
- Dutch Oven Lemon Bars
- Campfire Baked Apples
- Dutch Oven Cherry Cobbler
- Campfire Caramelized Bananas
- Dutch Oven Chocolate Chip Cookies
- Campfire Rice Krispie Treats
- Dutch Oven Mixed Berry Galette
- Campfire Chocolate Fondue
- Dutch Oven Peach Dumplings
- Camp Dutch Oven Berry Bread Pudding
- Dutch Oven Key Lime Pie
- Campfire Grilled Peaches
- Dutch Oven Cranberry Orange Bread

- Camp Dutch Oven Tiramisu
- Dutch Oven Apricot Crisp
- Campfire Cinnamon Sugar Donuts
- Dutch Oven Coconut Macaroons
- Camp Dutch Oven Berry Cobbler Bars
- Dutch Oven Lemon Poppy Seed Cake
- Campfire Apple Cider Doughnuts
- Dutch Oven Rhubarb Crisp
- Camp Dutch Oven Almond Joy Brownies
- Dutch Oven Cherry Chocolate Cake
- Campfire Caramel Apple Nachos
- Dutch Oven Butterscotch Pudding
- Camp Dutch Oven Peanut Butter Cup S'mores
- Dutch Oven Raspberry Cheesecake
- Campfire Trail Mix Bars

Dutch Oven Apple Crisp

Ingredients:

- 6 cups sliced apples (such as Granny Smith or Honeycrisp)
- 1 tablespoon lemon juice
- 1/2 cup granulated sugar
- 1 teaspoon ground cinnamon
- 1/4 teaspoon ground nutmeg
- 1 cup old-fashioned oats
- 1/2 cup all-purpose flour
- 1/2 cup packed brown sugar
- 1/2 cup unsalted butter, cold and diced
- Pinch of salt

Instructions:

Prepare the Dutch Oven:
- Preheat your Dutch oven by placing it over the campfire or on hot coals.

Prepare the Apples:
- In a large bowl, toss the sliced apples with lemon juice to prevent browning.
- Add granulated sugar, cinnamon, and nutmeg to the apples, and toss to coat evenly.

Make the Crisp Topping:
- In another bowl, combine oats, flour, brown sugar, and a pinch of salt.
- Cut in the cold diced butter using a pastry cutter or your fingers until the mixture resembles coarse crumbs.

Assemble the Crisp:
- Spread the seasoned sliced apples evenly in the preheated Dutch oven.
- Sprinkle the crisp topping over the apples, covering them completely.

Bake in the Dutch Oven:
- Place the lid on the Dutch oven and arrange hot coals on top of the lid to create an even heat source.
- Bake the apple crisp for about 30-40 minutes, or until the apples are tender and the topping is golden brown and crisp.

Serve:
- Remove the Dutch oven from the heat and let the apple crisp cool for a few minutes.

- Serve the apple crisp warm, either on its own or with a scoop of vanilla ice cream or whipped cream if desired.

This Dutch Oven Apple Crisp is a comforting and delicious camping dessert, perfect for enjoying around the campfire under the stars.

Campfire Peach Cobbler

Ingredients:

- 4 cups sliced fresh or canned peaches (if using canned, drain excess liquid)
- 1/2 cup granulated sugar
- 1 tablespoon lemon juice
- 1 teaspoon vanilla extract
- 1 cup all-purpose flour
- 1/2 cup granulated sugar
- 1 teaspoon baking powder
- 1/4 teaspoon salt
- 1/2 cup unsalted butter, melted
- 1/2 cup milk
- Ground cinnamon (optional)
- Whipped cream or vanilla ice cream for serving (optional)

Instructions:

Prepare the Campfire:
- Start a campfire and allow it to burn down until you have a bed of hot coals. You can also use a charcoal grill or a portable campfire grill.

Prepare the Dutch Oven:
- Grease the bottom and sides of a cast iron Dutch oven with butter or cooking spray.

Prepare the Peach Filling:
- In a bowl, combine the sliced peaches, 1/2 cup sugar, lemon juice, and vanilla extract. Stir well to coat the peaches evenly.

Make the Cobbler Batter:
- In another bowl, mix together the flour, 1/2 cup sugar, baking powder, and salt.
- Add the melted butter and milk to the dry ingredients, and stir until just combined. The batter will be thick and lumpy.

Assemble the Cobbler:
- Pour the peach mixture into the greased Dutch oven, spreading it out evenly.
- Spoon the cobbler batter over the peaches, spreading it out to cover the fruit as much as possible.

Cook Over the Campfire:

- Place the lid on the Dutch oven and position it over the hot coals of the campfire.
- Arrange some hot coals on top of the lid to create even heat distribution.
- Cook the peach cobbler for about 30-40 minutes, or until the topping is golden brown and the peach filling is bubbling.

Serve:
- Once the cobbler is cooked, carefully remove the Dutch oven from the heat.
- Allow the cobbler to cool for a few minutes before serving.
- Serve warm, sprinkled with ground cinnamon if desired, and top with whipped cream or vanilla ice cream for an extra indulgence.

Enjoy this delicious campfire peach cobbler as a sweet and comforting treat during your outdoor adventures!

Chocolate Lava Cake

Ingredients:

- 4 ounces semi-sweet chocolate (chopped)
- 1/2 cup unsalted butter
- 2 large eggs
- 2 large egg yolks
- 1/4 cup granulated sugar
- 2 teaspoons vanilla extract
- 1/4 cup all-purpose flour
- Pinch of salt
- Cooking spray or extra butter for greasing the Dutch oven

Instructions:

Preheat the Dutch Oven:
- If you're using a campfire, prepare the coals to medium heat. Place a rack or trivet inside the Dutch oven to elevate it slightly above the coals.

Prepare the Chocolate Mixture:
- In a heatproof bowl, combine the chopped chocolate and unsalted butter. Place the bowl over a pot of simmering water (or use a double boiler) and stir until melted and smooth. Remove from heat and let it cool slightly.

Prepare the Batter:
- In a separate mixing bowl, whisk together the eggs, egg yolks, granulated sugar, and vanilla extract until well combined.
- Gradually pour the melted chocolate mixture into the egg mixture, whisking constantly until smooth.
- Fold in the all-purpose flour and a pinch of salt until just combined. Be careful not to overmix.

Grease the Dutch Oven:
- Lightly grease the bottom and sides of the Dutch oven with cooking spray or butter to prevent sticking.

Fill the Dutch Oven:
- Pour the batter into the greased Dutch oven, spreading it out evenly.

Cooking:
- Place the Dutch oven onto the rack or trivet above the campfire coals.
- Cover the Dutch oven with its lid and add some hot coals on top for even heat distribution.

- Bake the chocolate lava cake for about 15-20 minutes or until the edges are set but the center is still slightly jiggly.

Serve:
- Carefully remove the Dutch oven from the heat and let it cool for a few minutes.
- Use a spoon to scoop out the chocolate lava cake onto serving plates.
- Serve immediately, either on its own or with a dollop of whipped cream or a scoop of vanilla ice cream.

Enjoy the rich and gooey center of this campfire chocolate lava cake, perfect for satisfying your sweet tooth while enjoying the great outdoors!

Camp Dutch Oven Brownies

Ingredients:

- 1 cup all-purpose flour
- 1 cup granulated sugar
- 1/2 cup unsweetened cocoa powder
- 1/2 teaspoon baking powder
- 1/2 teaspoon salt
- 2 large eggs
- 1/2 cup vegetable oil
- 1 teaspoon vanilla extract
- 1/2 cup chocolate chips (optional)
- Cooking spray or butter (for greasing the Dutch oven)

Instructions:

Prepare the Dutch Oven:
- Start by preparing your campfire. You'll want to have a good bed of hot coals.
- Grease the inside of your camp Dutch oven thoroughly with cooking spray or butter to prevent sticking.

Mix Dry Ingredients:
- In a mixing bowl, whisk together the flour, sugar, cocoa powder, baking powder, and salt until well combined.

Add Wet Ingredients:
- Add the eggs, vegetable oil, and vanilla extract to the dry ingredients. Mix until the batter is smooth and well incorporated.
- If desired, fold in chocolate chips for extra richness and flavor.

Transfer to Dutch Oven:
- Pour the brownie batter into the greased camp Dutch oven, spreading it out evenly.

Bake over Campfire:
- Place the Dutch oven over the hot coals of the campfire. Make sure to have some coals on top of the Dutch oven as well for even baking.
- Bake the brownies for about 20-25 minutes or until the edges are set and a toothpick inserted into the center comes out with moist crumbs (the center will continue to cook from residual heat).
- Rotate the Dutch oven occasionally to ensure even cooking.

Serve:

- Once the brownies are done, remove the Dutch oven from the heat and let the brownies cool slightly.
- Cut the brownies into squares and serve warm.
- Optionally, you can serve with a scoop of vanilla ice cream or whipped cream for an extra indulgent treat.

These camp Dutch oven brownies are sure to be a hit with your fellow campers. Enjoy the rich chocolate flavor and the warmth of the campfire as you indulge in this delicious camping dessert.

Pineapple Upside-Down Cake

Ingredients:

- 1/4 cup unsalted butter
- 3/4 cup packed brown sugar
- 7-8 canned pineapple rings
- Maraschino cherries, for garnish
- 1 1/2 cups all-purpose flour
- 1 1/2 teaspoons baking powder
- 1/4 teaspoon salt
- 1/2 cup unsalted butter, softened
- 3/4 cup granulated sugar
- 2 large eggs
- 1 teaspoon vanilla extract
- 1/2 cup milk

Instructions:

Prepare the Dutch Oven:
- Grease the inside of your camp Dutch oven thoroughly with cooking spray or butter.

Create the Topping:
- Melt 1/4 cup of unsalted butter in a small saucepan over medium heat.
- Add the brown sugar to the melted butter, stirring until it dissolves and becomes syrupy.
- Pour the syrup evenly into the bottom of the greased Dutch oven.

Arrange Pineapple and Cherries:
- Place the pineapple rings on top of the brown sugar syrup in a single layer.
- Put a maraschino cherry in the center of each pineapple ring and fill in any gaps with additional cherries.

Prepare the Cake Batter:
- In a medium mixing bowl, whisk together the flour, baking powder, and salt until well combined.
- In a separate large mixing bowl, cream together the softened butter and granulated sugar until light and fluffy.
- Beat in the eggs, one at a time, followed by the vanilla extract.
- Gradually add the dry ingredients to the wet ingredients, alternating with the milk, until a smooth batter forms.

Pour Batter Over Pineapples:

- Carefully pour the cake batter over the arranged pineapple slices and cherries in the Dutch oven, spreading it out evenly.

Bake over Campfire:
- Place the Dutch oven over the hot coals of the campfire. Make sure to have some coals on top of the Dutch oven as well for even baking.
- Bake the cake for about 30-40 minutes or until a toothpick inserted into the center comes out clean.

Cool and Serve:
- Once the cake is done, remove the Dutch oven from the heat and let it cool for a few minutes.
- Carefully invert the cake onto a serving platter or plate. Allow the cake to cool slightly before serving.

Enjoy this delicious Pineapple Upside-Down Cake warm, with the sweet caramelized pineapple topping and moist cake underneath. It's the perfect dessert for your camping adventures!

Dutch Oven Banana Bread

Ingredients:

- 2 cups all-purpose flour
- 1 teaspoon baking soda
- 1/4 teaspoon salt
- 1/2 cup unsalted butter, softened
- 3/4 cup granulated sugar
- 2 large eggs
- 3 ripe bananas, mashed
- 1/4 cup plain yogurt or sour cream
- 1 teaspoon vanilla extract
- 1/2 cup chopped nuts (optional)

Instructions:

Preheat Your Dutch Oven:
- If you're using charcoal briquettes, preheat about 20 charcoal briquettes until they are glowing and evenly hot. If you're using a campfire, make sure you have a good bed of hot coals.

Prepare the Dutch Oven:
- Grease the inside of your Dutch oven with cooking spray or butter to prevent sticking.

Mix Dry Ingredients:
- In a bowl, whisk together the flour, baking soda, and salt until well combined.

Cream Butter and Sugar:
- In a separate large mixing bowl, cream together the softened butter and granulated sugar until light and fluffy.

Add Wet Ingredients:
- Beat in the eggs, one at a time, until well incorporated.
- Mix in the mashed bananas, yogurt or sour cream, and vanilla extract until smooth.

Combine Wet and Dry Ingredients:
- Gradually add the dry ingredients to the wet ingredients, mixing until just combined. Be careful not to overmix.
- If using chopped nuts, fold them into the batter at this stage.

Transfer Batter to Dutch Oven:
- Pour the batter into the greased Dutch oven, spreading it out evenly.

Bake in Dutch Oven:
- Place the Dutch oven over the hot coals of the campfire or charcoal briquettes. Make sure to have some coals on top of the Dutch oven as well for even baking.
- Bake the banana bread for about 45-55 minutes, or until a toothpick inserted into the center comes out clean.

Cool and Serve:
- Once the banana bread is done, remove the Dutch oven from the heat and let it cool for a few minutes.
- Carefully remove the banana bread from the Dutch oven and let it cool completely on a wire rack before slicing and serving.

Enjoy your delicious Dutch Oven Banana Bread as a delightful treat during your camping adventures!

Campfire S'mores Dip

Ingredients:

- 1 cup chocolate chips (milk chocolate or semi-sweet)
- 1 cup mini marshmallows
- Graham crackers, for serving

Instructions:

Prepare Your Campfire:
- Start by setting up your campfire and allowing it to burn down until you have a good bed of hot coals.

Assemble the Dip:
- Take a cast iron skillet or a heatproof dish suitable for use over a campfire.
- Spread the chocolate chips evenly across the bottom of the skillet.
- Scatter the mini marshmallows on top of the chocolate chips, covering them completely.

Heat Over the Campfire:
- Carefully place the skillet over the hot coals of the campfire. Make sure the skillet is stable and won't tip over.
- Let the dip cook over the campfire, keeping a close eye on it to prevent burning. The heat from the coals will melt the chocolate and toast the marshmallows.

Serve:
- Once the chocolate is melted and the marshmallows are golden brown and gooey, remove the skillet from the campfire.
- Serve the s'mores dip immediately with graham crackers for dipping.

Enjoy:
- Invite everyone to gather around and dip their graham crackers into the warm and gooey s'mores dip.
- Be careful as the dip will be hot. Allow it to cool slightly before digging in!

Campfire S'mores Dip is a fun and interactive way to enjoy the flavors of s'mores without the hassle of assembling individual sandwiches. It's perfect for sharing with friends and family on your camping adventures!

Blueberry Lemon Dump Cake

Ingredients:

- 1 box (about 18.25 ounces) lemon cake mix
- 1 can (21 ounces) blueberry pie filling
- 1/2 cup unsalted butter, melted
- Zest of 1 lemon (optional)
- Cooking spray or butter (for greasing the Dutch oven)

Instructions:

Preheat Your Dutch Oven:
- If you're using charcoal briquettes, preheat about 20 charcoal briquettes until they are glowing and evenly hot. If you're using a campfire, make sure you have a good bed of hot coals.

Prepare the Dutch Oven:
- Grease the inside of your Dutch oven thoroughly with cooking spray or butter to prevent sticking.

Layer Ingredients:
- Spread the blueberry pie filling evenly on the bottom of the greased Dutch oven.
- Sprinkle the lemon cake mix evenly over the blueberry pie filling.
- Drizzle the melted butter over the cake mix, covering it as evenly as possible.
- If using, sprinkle lemon zest over the top for added flavor.

Bake in Dutch Oven:
- Place the Dutch oven over the hot coals of the campfire or charcoal briquettes. Make sure to have some coals on top of the Dutch oven as well for even baking.
- Bake the dump cake for about 30-40 minutes, or until the cake is golden brown and the blueberry filling is bubbling around the edges.

Cool and Serve:
- Once the dump cake is done, remove the Dutch oven from the heat and let it cool for a few minutes.
- Serve the dump cake warm, either on its own or with a dollop of whipped cream or a scoop of vanilla ice cream if desired.

Enjoy this delicious Blueberry Lemon Dump Cake as a sweet and tangy treat during your camping adventures!

Dutch Oven Cherry Clafoutis

Ingredients:

- 1 pound fresh cherries, pitted
- 3/4 cup granulated sugar
- 3 large eggs
- 1 cup milk
- 1/2 cup all-purpose flour
- 1 teaspoon vanilla extract
- Pinch of salt
- Powdered sugar, for dusting (optional)
- Cooking spray or butter (for greasing the Dutch oven)

Instructions:

Preheat Your Dutch Oven:
- If you're using charcoal briquettes, preheat about 20 charcoal briquettes until they are glowing and evenly hot. If you're using a campfire, make sure you have a good bed of hot coals.

Prepare the Dutch Oven:
- Grease the inside of your Dutch oven thoroughly with cooking spray or butter to prevent sticking.

Arrange Cherries:
- Spread the pitted cherries evenly on the bottom of the greased Dutch oven.

Mix Batter:
- In a mixing bowl, whisk together the granulated sugar and eggs until well combined.
- Gradually whisk in the milk until smooth.
- Stir in the flour, vanilla extract, and a pinch of salt until you have a smooth batter.

Pour Batter Over Cherries:
- Pour the batter over the arranged cherries in the Dutch oven, covering them evenly.

Bake in Dutch Oven:
- Place the Dutch oven over the hot coals of the campfire or charcoal briquettes. Make sure to have some coals on top of the Dutch oven as well for even baking.

- Bake the clafoutis for about 30-40 minutes, or until the top is golden brown and the center is set.

Cool and Serve:
- Once the clafoutis is done, remove the Dutch oven from the heat and let it cool for a few minutes.
- Dust the clafoutis with powdered sugar if desired.
- Serve the clafoutis warm or at room temperature, either on its own or with a dollop of whipped cream or vanilla ice cream.

Enjoy this delicious Dutch Oven Cherry Clafoutis as a delightful and elegant dessert during your camping adventures!

Cinnamon Roll Campfire Bake

Ingredients:

- 1 can (about 8 ounces) refrigerated cinnamon rolls with icing
- 1/4 cup unsalted butter, melted
- 1/4 cup packed brown sugar
- 1 teaspoon ground cinnamon
- Cooking spray or butter (for greasing the Dutch oven)

Instructions:

Preheat Your Dutch Oven:
- If you're using charcoal briquettes, preheat about 20 charcoal briquettes until they are glowing and evenly hot. If you're using a campfire, make sure you have a good bed of hot coals.

Prepare the Dutch Oven:
- Grease the inside of your Dutch oven thoroughly with cooking spray or butter to prevent sticking.

Prepare the Cinnamon Roll Dough:
- Open the can of refrigerated cinnamon rolls and separate them into individual rolls.
- Cut each cinnamon roll into quarters.

Create the Cinnamon Roll Layers:
- In a small bowl, mix together the melted butter, brown sugar, and ground cinnamon until well combined.
- Dip each quartered cinnamon roll piece into the butter mixture, coating it thoroughly.
- Arrange the coated cinnamon roll pieces in an even layer at the bottom of the greased Dutch oven.

Bake in Dutch Oven:
- Place the Dutch oven over the hot coals of the campfire or charcoal briquettes. Make sure to have some coals on top of the Dutch oven as well for even baking.
- Bake the cinnamon roll bake for about 20-25 minutes, or until the cinnamon rolls are golden brown and cooked through.

Cool and Serve:
- Once the cinnamon roll bake is done, remove the Dutch oven from the heat and let it cool for a few minutes.

- Drizzle the icing from the refrigerated cinnamon roll package over the top of the warm cinnamon roll bake.
- Serve the cinnamon roll bake warm and enjoy the gooey, cinnamon-sugar goodness!

This Cinnamon Roll Campfire Bake is a delicious and comforting treat that's perfect for breakfast or dessert during your camping adventures.

Dutch Oven Strawberry Shortcake

Ingredients:

- 2 cups all-purpose flour
- 1/4 cup granulated sugar
- 1 tablespoon baking powder
- 1/2 teaspoon salt
- 1/2 cup unsalted butter, cold and diced
- 3/4 cup milk
- 1 teaspoon vanilla extract
- 4 cups fresh strawberries, hulled and sliced
- 1/4 cup granulated sugar (for macerating strawberries)
- Whipped cream or vanilla ice cream, for serving

Instructions:

Preheat Your Dutch Oven:
- If you're using charcoal briquettes, preheat about 20 charcoal briquettes until they are glowing and evenly hot. If you're using a campfire, make sure you have a good bed of hot coals.

Prepare the Strawberries:
- In a bowl, combine the sliced strawberries with 1/4 cup of granulated sugar. Stir to coat the strawberries evenly, then set aside to macerate while you prepare the shortcake.

Prepare the Shortcake Dough:
- In a large mixing bowl, whisk together the flour, 1/4 cup of granulated sugar, baking powder, and salt.
- Cut in the cold diced butter using a pastry cutter or your fingers until the mixture resembles coarse crumbs.
- In a separate small bowl, mix together the milk and vanilla extract.
- Gradually add the milk mixture to the dry ingredients, stirring until a soft dough forms.

Form Shortcake:
- Turn the dough out onto a lightly floured surface and knead gently a few times until it comes together.
- Pat the dough into a circle about 1 inch thick.

Bake in Dutch Oven:
- Place the shortcake dough into the greased Dutch oven.

- Cover the Dutch oven with its lid and place it over the hot coals or charcoal briquettes.
- Bake the shortcake for about 20-25 minutes, or until it is golden brown and cooked through.

Assemble Strawberry Shortcake:
- Once the shortcake is done, remove it from the Dutch oven and let it cool slightly.
- Cut the shortcake into wedges and split each wedge horizontally.
- Spoon some of the macerated strawberries over the bottom half of each shortcake wedge.
- Top with a dollop of whipped cream or a scoop of vanilla ice cream.
- Place the top half of the shortcake over the strawberries and cream.
- Serve immediately and enjoy your delicious Dutch Oven Strawberry Shortcake!

This Dutch Oven Strawberry Shortcake is a delightful and classic dessert that's perfect for enjoying around the campfire with friends and family.

Camp Dutch Oven Pineapple Cake

Ingredients:

- 1 can (20 ounces) crushed pineapple, undrained
- 1 box (about 18.25 ounces) yellow cake mix
- 1/2 cup unsalted butter, melted
- Cooking spray or butter (for greasing the Dutch oven)

Instructions:

Preheat Your Dutch Oven:
- If you're using charcoal briquettes, preheat about 20 charcoal briquettes until they are glowing and evenly hot. If you're using a campfire, make sure you have a good bed of hot coals.

Prepare the Dutch Oven:
- Grease the inside of your Dutch oven thoroughly with cooking spray or butter to prevent sticking.

Layer Ingredients:
- Spread the crushed pineapple (including the juice) evenly on the bottom of the greased Dutch oven.

Prepare Cake Mix:
- In a mixing bowl, prepare the yellow cake mix according to the package instructions.

Pour Cake Batter Over Pineapple:
- Pour the prepared cake batter over the crushed pineapple in the Dutch oven, spreading it out evenly.

Drizzle Melted Butter:
- Drizzle the melted butter over the top of the cake batter, covering it as evenly as possible.

Bake in Dutch Oven:
- Place the Dutch oven over the hot coals of the campfire or charcoal briquettes. Make sure to have some coals on top of the Dutch oven as well for even baking.
- Bake the pineapple cake for about 30-40 minutes, or until the cake is golden brown and cooked through.

Cool and Serve:
- Once the cake is done, remove the Dutch oven from the heat and let it cool for a few minutes.

- Serve the pineapple cake warm, either on its own or with a dollop of whipped cream or a scoop of vanilla ice cream if desired.

This Camp Dutch Oven Pineapple Cake is a delicious and easy dessert that's perfect for enjoying during your camping adventures. The combination of sweet pineapple and moist cake is sure to be a hit with your fellow campers!

Blackberry Cobbler

Ingredients:

- 6 cups fresh blackberries
- 1 cup granulated sugar
- 1 tablespoon lemon juice
- 1 cup all-purpose flour
- 1 cup granulated sugar
- 1 teaspoon baking powder
- 1/4 teaspoon salt
- 1/2 cup unsalted butter, melted
- 1/2 cup milk
- 1 teaspoon vanilla extract

Instructions:

Preheat Your Dutch Oven:
- If you're using charcoal briquettes, preheat about 20 charcoal briquettes until they are glowing and evenly hot. If you're using a campfire, make sure you have a good bed of hot coals.

Prepare the Dutch Oven:
- Grease the inside of your Dutch oven thoroughly with cooking spray or butter to prevent sticking.

Prepare the Blackberries:
- In a large bowl, combine the fresh blackberries, 1 cup of granulated sugar, and lemon juice. Toss gently to coat the blackberries evenly with the sugar. Let them sit for about 15 minutes to macerate.

Make the Cobbler Batter:
- In another mixing bowl, whisk together the flour, 1 cup of granulated sugar, baking powder, and salt until well combined.
- Stir in the melted butter, milk, and vanilla extract until a smooth batter forms.

Assemble the Cobbler:
- Pour the macerated blackberries into the bottom of the greased Dutch oven, spreading them out evenly.
- Spoon the cobbler batter over the blackberries, spreading it out evenly to cover them.

Bake in Dutch Oven:

- Place the Dutch oven over the hot coals of the campfire or charcoal briquettes. Make sure to have some coals on top of the Dutch oven as well for even baking.
- Bake the blackberry cobbler for about 30-40 minutes, or until the cobbler is golden brown and the blackberry filling is bubbling around the edges.

Cool and Serve:
- Once the cobbler is done, remove the Dutch oven from the heat and let it cool for a few minutes.
- Serve the blackberry cobbler warm, either on its own or with a scoop of vanilla ice cream or a dollop of whipped cream if desired.

This Camp Dutch Oven Blackberry Cobbler is a delicious and comforting dessert that's perfect for enjoying around the campfire with friends and family.

Dutch Oven Pecan Pie

Ingredients:

- 1 prepared pie crust (homemade or store-bought)
- 1 cup pecan halves
- 3 large eggs
- 1 cup light corn syrup
- 1/2 cup granulated sugar
- 1/4 cup unsalted butter, melted
- 1 teaspoon vanilla extract
- 1/4 teaspoon salt

Instructions:

Preheat Your Dutch Oven:
- If you're using charcoal briquettes, preheat about 20 charcoal briquettes until they are glowing and evenly hot. If you're using a campfire, make sure you have a good bed of hot coals.

Prepare the Dutch Oven:
- Grease the inside of your Dutch oven thoroughly with cooking spray or butter to prevent sticking.

Line the Dutch Oven with Pie Crust:
- Place the prepared pie crust in the greased Dutch oven, pressing it gently to fit the bottom and up the sides.

Arrange Pecans:
- Scatter the pecan halves evenly over the bottom of the pie crust.

Prepare the Filling:
- In a mixing bowl, whisk together the eggs, corn syrup, granulated sugar, melted butter, vanilla extract, and salt until well combined.

Pour Filling Over Pecans:
- Pour the pecan pie filling over the pecans in the pie crust, making sure it's evenly distributed.

Bake in Dutch Oven:
- Place the Dutch oven over the hot coals of the campfire or charcoal briquettes. Make sure to have some coals on top of the Dutch oven as well for even baking.
- Bake the pecan pie for about 40-50 minutes, or until the filling is set and the crust is golden brown.

Cool and Serve:

- Once the pecan pie is done, remove the Dutch oven from the heat and let it cool for a few minutes.
- Serve the pecan pie warm, either on its own or with a dollop of whipped cream or a scoop of vanilla ice cream if desired.

This Dutch Oven Pecan Pie is a delicious and indulgent dessert that's perfect for enjoying around the campfire with friends and family.

Campfire Monkey Bread

Ingredients:

- 2 cans (16.3 ounces each) refrigerated biscuit dough
- 1 cup granulated sugar
- 2 teaspoons ground cinnamon
- 1/2 cup (1 stick) unsalted butter, melted
- 1/2 cup brown sugar
- Cooking spray

Instructions:

Prepare the Campfire:
- If you're camping, you'll need a campfire with hot coals. If you're doing this in your backyard or somewhere with a grill, you can use a grill with a grate positioned over hot coals.

Prepare the Bundt Pan:
- Spray the inside of a Bundt pan with cooking spray to prevent sticking.

Prep the Dough:
- Open the biscuit cans and separate the dough into individual biscuits.
- Cut each biscuit into quarters.

Coat the Dough:
- In a large zip-top bag, combine the granulated sugar and cinnamon. Add the biscuit pieces to the bag, seal it, and shake to coat the dough evenly with the cinnamon-sugar mixture.

Arrange in the Pan:
- Layer the coated biscuit pieces into the prepared Bundt pan.

Make the Sauce:
- In a small bowl, mix the melted butter and brown sugar until well combined.

Pour Sauce Over the Dough:
- Pour the butter and brown sugar mixture evenly over the biscuit pieces in the Bundt pan.

Wrap in Foil:
- Cover the Bundt pan with aluminum foil.

Cook Over the Campfire:
- Place the Bundt pan on a grate positioned over hot coals.
- Cook for about 25-30 minutes, rotating the pan occasionally to ensure even cooking.

- The monkey bread is done when it's golden brown and bubbling.

Serve:
- Carefully remove the foil from the Bundt pan.
- Allow the monkey bread to cool for a few minutes before inverting it onto a serving plate.
- Serve warm and enjoy!

Campfire Monkey Bread is a delicious treat that's sure to be a hit with everyone around the campfire. It's gooey, sweet, and perfect for sharing with friends and family.

Dutch Oven Bread Pudding

Ingredients:

- 6 cups of day-old bread (such as French bread or brioche), cubed
- 4 large eggs
- 2 cups whole milk
- 1/2 cup heavy cream
- 1/2 cup granulated sugar
- 1/4 cup brown sugar
- 1 teaspoon vanilla extract
- 1 teaspoon ground cinnamon
- 1/4 teaspoon ground nutmeg
- Pinch of salt
- 1/2 cup raisins or other dried fruit (optional)
- Butter, for greasing the Dutch oven

Instructions:

Prepare the Dutch Oven:
- Grease the bottom and sides of a 10-inch Dutch oven with butter.

Prepare the Bread:
- Cut the day-old bread into cubes and spread them evenly in the greased Dutch oven.

Make the Custard Mixture:
- In a large mixing bowl, whisk together the eggs, milk, heavy cream, granulated sugar, brown sugar, vanilla extract, cinnamon, nutmeg, and a pinch of salt until well combined.

Pour Custard Over Bread:
- Pour the custard mixture over the bread cubes in the Dutch oven, making sure to coat all the bread evenly. If using raisins or other dried fruit, sprinkle them over the bread mixture.

Let it Soak:
- Press down gently on the bread with a spatula or spoon to help the bread soak up the custard mixture.

Preheat the Dutch Oven:
- Place the Dutch oven over hot coals or on a grill with hot coals underneath. Allow it to preheat for about 10 minutes.

Bake:

- Once preheated, cover the Dutch oven with its lid and place some hot coals on top of the lid.
- Bake for about 30-40 minutes, or until the bread pudding is set and golden brown on top. You can check for doneness by inserting a knife into the center – it should come out clean when the bread pudding is ready.

Serve:
- Carefully remove the Dutch oven from the heat and let the bread pudding cool slightly.
- Serve warm, optionally topped with whipped cream or a drizzle of caramel sauce.

This Dutch Oven Bread Pudding is a comforting and indulgent dessert that's perfect for outdoor gatherings or camping trips. Enjoy the rich flavors and cozy warmth it brings!

Orange Campfire Cake

Ingredients:

- 1 box of yellow cake mix (plus ingredients listed on the box, typically eggs, oil, and water)
- 3 large oranges
- Cooking spray or butter for greasing

Optional Toppings:

- Powdered sugar
- Whipped cream
- Fresh berries

Instructions:

    Prepare the Cake Batter:
- Follow the instructions on the box of yellow cake mix to prepare the batter. This usually involves combining the cake mix with eggs, oil, and water in a mixing bowl.

    Prepare the Oranges:
- Slice off the tops of the oranges and set them aside. Be careful not to cut through the bottom of the oranges.
- Use a spoon to scoop out the flesh of the oranges, leaving just the peel intact. You can save the scooped-out orange segments for snacking or juice.

    Fill the Orange Peels:
- Spray the inside of each orange peel with cooking spray or rub them with butter to prevent sticking.
- Fill each orange peel about two-thirds full with the prepared cake batter.

    Replace the Tops:
- Place the orange tops back onto the filled oranges. They will act as lids during cooking.

    Wrap in Foil:
- Wrap each filled orange individually in aluminum foil, making sure they are tightly sealed.

    Cook Over the Campfire:
- Place the foil-wrapped oranges directly onto the hot coals of your campfire.

- Cook for about 20-30 minutes, rotating them occasionally to ensure even cooking. The cakes are done when a toothpick inserted into the center comes out clean.

Serve:
- Carefully unwrap the foil from each orange and remove the tops.
- Optionally, dust the cakes with powdered sugar and serve with whipped cream and fresh berries on the side.

This orange campfire cake is a fun and delicious dessert that's perfect for camping trips or outdoor gatherings. Enjoy the moist and flavorful cake with a hint of citrus zest!

Dutch Oven Berry Crumble

Ingredients:

- 4 cups mixed berries (such as strawberries, blueberries, raspberries, blackberries)
- 1/2 cup granulated sugar (adjust according to the sweetness of the berries)
- 1 tablespoon cornstarch
- 1 tablespoon lemon juice
- 1 cup old-fashioned rolled oats
- 1/2 cup all-purpose flour
- 1/2 cup brown sugar
- 1/2 cup unsalted butter, cold and cubed
- 1 teaspoon ground cinnamon
- Pinch of salt
- Cooking spray or butter for greasing the Dutch oven

Optional Toppings:

- Vanilla ice cream
- Whipped cream

Instructions:

Prepare the Dutch Oven:
- Grease the bottom and sides of a 10-inch Dutch oven with cooking spray or butter.

Prepare the Berry Filling:
- In a mixing bowl, combine the mixed berries, granulated sugar, cornstarch, and lemon juice. Toss until the berries are evenly coated. Transfer the berry mixture to the greased Dutch oven.

Prepare the Crumble Topping:
- In another mixing bowl, combine the rolled oats, all-purpose flour, brown sugar, cubed unsalted butter, ground cinnamon, and a pinch of salt.
- Use your fingers or a pastry cutter to mix the ingredients together until the mixture resembles coarse crumbs.

Assemble and Cook:
- Sprinkle the crumble topping evenly over the berry mixture in the Dutch oven.

Bake:

- Place the lid on the Dutch oven.
- Arrange hot coals in a circle on the ground or on a grill, and place the Dutch oven on top of the hot coals.
- Place some hot coals on top of the lid.
- Bake for about 30-40 minutes, or until the berry filling is bubbling and the crumble topping is golden brown and crisp. Check occasionally to avoid burning.

Serve:
- Carefully remove the Dutch oven from the heat.
- Serve the berry crumble warm, optionally topped with vanilla ice cream or whipped cream.

This Dutch Oven Berry Crumble is a delightful dessert that showcases the sweetness of fresh berries with a crunchy, buttery topping. Enjoy it as a comforting treat during your outdoor adventures!

Campfire Peach Melba

Ingredients:

- 4 ripe peaches, halved and pitted
- 1 cup fresh raspberries
- 1/4 cup granulated sugar (adjust to taste depending on the sweetness of the fruit)
- 1 tablespoon lemon juice
- 1 teaspoon vanilla extract
- 1/2 cup crushed graham crackers or biscuit crumbs
- Whipped cream or vanilla ice cream for serving (optional)
- Aluminum foil

Instructions:

Prepare the Campfire:
- Start by building a campfire and letting it burn down until you have a good amount of hot coals.

Prepare the Peach Halves:
- Place each peach half, cut side up, on a piece of aluminum foil large enough to wrap it.
- In the hollow of each peach half, add a few fresh raspberries.

Sweeten and Flavor:
- Sprinkle the granulated sugar over the raspberries and peach halves.
- Drizzle each peach half with lemon juice and vanilla extract.

Wrap and Seal:
- Fold the aluminum foil around each peach half, creating a sealed packet.

Cook Over the Campfire:
- Place the foil-wrapped peach halves directly onto the hot coals of the campfire.
- Cook for about 15-20 minutes, or until the peaches are tender and juicy. You can rotate them occasionally for even cooking.

Serve:
- Carefully remove the foil packets from the campfire and let them cool for a few minutes.
- Open the foil packets and transfer the peach halves to serving plates.
- Sprinkle each peach half with crushed graham crackers or biscuit crumbs.
- Optionally, serve with a dollop of whipped cream or a scoop of vanilla ice cream on top.

Campfire Peach Melba is best enjoyed warm, with the juices from the peaches and raspberries mingling together with the sweet crumbs. It's a simple yet delicious dessert that's perfect for camping trips or outdoor gatherings.

Dutch Oven Pumpkin Pie

Ingredients:

For the Pie Crust:

- 1 1/4 cups all-purpose flour
- 1/2 teaspoon salt
- 1/2 teaspoon granulated sugar
- 1/2 cup (1 stick) cold unsalted butter, cut into small pieces
- 2-4 tablespoons ice water

For the Filling:

- 1 can (15 ounces) pumpkin puree
- 3/4 cup granulated sugar
- 2 large eggs
- 1 teaspoon ground cinnamon
- 1/2 teaspoon ground ginger
- 1/4 teaspoon ground nutmeg
- 1/4 teaspoon ground cloves
- 1/2 teaspoon salt
- 1 can (12 ounces) evaporated milk

Equipment:

- 10-inch Dutch oven with lid
- Aluminum foil

Instructions:

Making the Pie Crust:

> In a large mixing bowl, combine the flour, salt, and sugar.
> Add the cold butter pieces to the flour mixture. Using a pastry cutter or your fingertips, cut the butter into the flour until the mixture resembles coarse crumbs.
> Gradually add the ice water, 1 tablespoon at a time, mixing gently with a fork, until the dough comes together and forms a ball.
> Shape the dough into a disc, wrap it in plastic wrap, and refrigerate for at least 30 minutes.

Preparing the Dutch Oven:

Prepare your campfire by building a bed of hot coals.

Making the Filling:

In a large mixing bowl, combine the pumpkin puree, granulated sugar, eggs, cinnamon, ginger, nutmeg, cloves, and salt. Mix until well combined.
Gradually stir in the evaporated milk until the mixture is smooth and uniform.

Assembling and Baking the Pie:

Remove the chilled pie dough from the refrigerator and roll it out on a lightly floured surface to fit the bottom and sides of your Dutch oven.
Carefully line the bottom and sides of the Dutch oven with the pie crust dough, trimming any excess.
Pour the pumpkin filling into the prepared pie crust.
Cover the Dutch oven with its lid. If the lid has a rim, you can fill it with hot coals.
Place the Dutch oven over the hot coals of your campfire, making sure to distribute the heat evenly.
Bake the pie for about 45-60 minutes, or until the filling is set and the crust is golden brown. You can check for doneness by inserting a knife into the center – it should come out clean when the pie is ready.
If the crust is browning too quickly, you can place a few layers of aluminum foil over the top to prevent burning.

Serving:

Once the pie is done baking, carefully remove the Dutch oven from the heat and let it cool for a few minutes.
Slice and serve the Dutch Oven Pumpkin Pie warm or at room temperature.

Enjoy your delicious Dutch Oven Pumpkin Pie with whipped cream or ice cream if desired. It's the perfect dessert for fall camping trips or outdoor gatherings!

Camp Dutch Oven Apple Fritters

Ingredients:

- 2 cups all-purpose flour
- 2 teaspoons baking powder
- 1/2 teaspoon salt
- 1/4 cup granulated sugar
- 1 teaspoon ground cinnamon
- 2 large eggs
- 1 cup milk
- 2 tablespoons melted butter
- 2 cups diced apples (peeled and cored)
- Vegetable oil for frying
- Powdered sugar for dusting
- Maple syrup (optional, for serving)

Instructions:

Prepare the Batter:
- In a large mixing bowl, combine the flour, baking powder, salt, sugar, and ground cinnamon.

Add Wet Ingredients:
- In a separate bowl, whisk together the eggs, milk, and melted butter.
- Pour the wet ingredients into the dry ingredients and mix until just combined. The batter may be slightly lumpy.

Fold in Apples:
- Gently fold in the diced apples until they are evenly distributed throughout the batter.

Preheat the Dutch Oven:
- Place a camp Dutch oven over hot coals to preheat. Add enough vegetable oil to cover the bottom with about an inch of oil.

Fry the Fritters:
- Once the oil is hot (around 350°F/175°C), use a spoon to drop spoonfuls of batter into the hot oil, making sure not to overcrowd the Dutch oven.
- Cook the fritters for about 2-3 minutes on each side, or until they are golden brown and crispy.
- Use tongs to carefully flip the fritters halfway through cooking.

Drain and Serve:

- Once the fritters are cooked, use a slotted spoon to transfer them to a plate lined with paper towels to drain any excess oil.
- Repeat the frying process with the remaining batter until all the fritters are cooked.

Serve:
- Dust the warm fritters with powdered sugar just before serving.
- Optionally, serve with maple syrup for dipping or drizzling.

These Camp Dutch Oven Apple Fritters are best enjoyed fresh and warm, with a crispy exterior and tender, apple-studded interior. They make for a delightful breakfast or dessert for any outdoor adventure.

Campfire Nutella S'mores

Ingredients:

- Graham crackers, broken into squares
- Nutella (or any hazelnut chocolate spread)
- Marshmallows

Instructions:

    Prepare the Campfire:
- Build a campfire and let it burn down until you have a good bed of hot coals.

    Assemble the S'mores:
- Take one graham cracker square and spread a generous amount of Nutella onto it.
- Place a marshmallow on top of the Nutella.

    Roast the Marshmallow:
- Hold the marshmallow over the hot coals using a skewer or roasting stick.
- Rotate the marshmallow slowly to ensure even roasting, until it becomes golden brown and gooey.

    Assemble the S'mores:
- Once the marshmallow is toasted to your liking, carefully place it on top of another graham cracker square.
- Press down gently to sandwich the marshmallow between the graham crackers and spread the Nutella.

    Enjoy:
- Repeat the process to make as many Nutella S'mores as desired.
- Serve immediately while the marshmallows are still warm and gooey.

These Campfire Nutella S'mores are a decadent and satisfying treat that's sure to be a hit with both kids and adults around the campfire. Enjoy the irresistible combination of chocolate-hazelnut spread, gooey marshmallows, and crunchy graham crackers!

Dutch Oven Lemon Bars

Ingredients:

For the Crust:

- 1 1/2 cups all-purpose flour
- 1/2 cup powdered sugar
- 3/4 cup unsalted butter, cold and cubed

For the Lemon Filling:

- 1 1/2 cups granulated sugar
- 1/4 cup all-purpose flour
- 4 large eggs
- 2/3 cup fresh lemon juice (about 3-4 lemons)
- Zest of 2 lemons
- Powdered sugar, for dusting (optional)

Instructions:

Prepare the Dutch Oven:
- Preheat your Dutch oven by placing it over hot coals, with additional coals on top to evenly distribute heat. Make sure it's well-greased to prevent sticking.

Prepare the Crust:
- In a mixing bowl, combine the flour and powdered sugar.
- Cut in the cold cubed butter using a pastry cutter or fork until the mixture resembles coarse crumbs.
- Press the mixture evenly into the bottom of the greased Dutch oven to form the crust.

Bake the Crust:
- Place the Dutch oven with the crust inside over the hot coals and bake for about 15-20 minutes, or until the crust is lightly golden brown.

Prepare the Lemon Filling:
- In a separate bowl, whisk together the granulated sugar and flour.
- Add the eggs, lemon juice, and lemon zest to the sugar mixture, and whisk until well combined and smooth.

Pour Filling Over Crust:

- Once the crust is baked, carefully pour the lemon filling over the hot crust, spreading it evenly.

Bake the Lemon Bars:
- Return the Dutch oven to the hot coals, cover with the lid, and bake for another 20-25 minutes, or until the filling is set and the edges are slightly golden brown.

Cool and Serve:
- Remove the Dutch oven from the heat and let the lemon bars cool completely.
- Once cooled, dust the top with powdered sugar if desired, then slice into bars and serve.

These Dutch Oven Lemon Bars are a delightful combination of sweet and tangy flavors, perfect for enjoying around the campfire or as a refreshing treat on any outdoor adventure.

Campfire Baked Apples

Ingredients:

- 4 large apples (such as Granny Smith or Honeycrisp)
- 1/4 cup brown sugar
- 1 teaspoon ground cinnamon
- 1/4 teaspoon ground nutmeg
- 2 tablespoons butter, diced
- 1/4 cup chopped nuts (such as walnuts or pecans), optional
- Raisins or dried cranberries, optional
- Vanilla ice cream or whipped cream, for serving (optional)

Instructions:

Prepare the Apples:
- Wash and core the apples, leaving the bottom intact so they can hold the filling.

Mix the Filling:
- In a small bowl, combine the brown sugar, cinnamon, and nutmeg.

Fill the Apples:
- Stuff each cored apple with the brown sugar mixture, dividing it evenly among them.
- If desired, add a few pieces of diced butter on top of the filling in each apple.
- Optionally, sprinkle chopped nuts and raisins or dried cranberries over the filling.

Wrap in Foil:
- Individually wrap each stuffed apple tightly in aluminum foil, making sure they are well sealed.

Cook Over the Campfire:
- Place the foil-wrapped apples directly onto the hot coals of the campfire.
- Cook for about 20-30 minutes, or until the apples are tender when pierced with a fork.

Serve:
- Carefully remove the foil-wrapped apples from the campfire.
- Unwrap the apples and transfer them to serving plates.
- Serve the campfire baked apples warm, optionally topped with a scoop of vanilla ice cream or whipped cream.

These campfire baked apples are sweet, tender, and bursting with flavor, making them a delightful dessert to enjoy outdoors. The combination of warm spices and gooey filling is sure to be a hit with everyone around the campfire.

Dutch Oven Cherry Cobbler

Ingredients:

- 6 medium-sized apples (such as Granny Smith or Honeycrisp)
- 1/2 cup brown sugar
- 1 teaspoon ground cinnamon
- 1/4 cup chopped nuts (such as walnuts or pecans)
- 1/4 cup raisins or dried cranberries
- 2 tablespoons butter, softened
- Optional toppings: vanilla ice cream, whipped cream, caramel sauce

Instructions:

Prepare the Campfire:
- Start by building a campfire and allowing it to burn down until you have hot coals.

Prepare the Apples:
- Core each apple, removing the seeds and creating a hollow space in the center.
- Score around the middle of each apple with a sharp knife to prevent them from bursting while cooking.

Make the Filling:
- In a small bowl, mix together the brown sugar, cinnamon, chopped nuts, and raisins or dried cranberries.

Fill the Apples:
- Stuff each cored apple with the filling mixture, pressing it gently into the cavities.
- Top each apple with a small piece of softened butter.

Wrap in Foil:
- Individually wrap each stuffed apple in aluminum foil, ensuring they are tightly sealed.

Cook Over the Campfire:
- Place the foil-wrapped apples directly onto the hot coals of the campfire.
- Cook for about 20-30 minutes, or until the apples are tender when pierced with a fork.

Serve:
- Carefully unwrap the foil from each apple and transfer them to serving plates.

- Optionally, serve with a scoop of vanilla ice cream, a dollop of whipped cream, or a drizzle of caramel sauce on top.

Campfire Baked Apples are a comforting and delicious dessert that's perfect for enjoying around the campfire. The warm, tender apples filled with sweet and nutty flavors are sure to be a hit with everyone!

Campfire Caramelized Bananas

Ingredients:

- 4 ripe bananas, peeled and sliced lengthwise
- 1/4 cup brown sugar
- 2 tablespoons unsalted butter, melted
- 1 teaspoon ground cinnamon
- Pinch of salt
- Optional toppings: chopped nuts, chocolate chips, whipped cream, vanilla ice cream

Instructions:

Prepare the Campfire:
- Start by building a campfire and allowing it to burn down until you have hot coals.

Prepare the Bananas:
- Slice the bananas lengthwise, leaving the peel on.

Make the Caramel Sauce:
- In a small bowl, mix together the brown sugar, melted butter, ground cinnamon, and a pinch of salt until well combined.

Coat the Bananas:
- Place the sliced bananas on a large piece of aluminum foil.
- Drizzle the caramel sauce over the bananas, making sure they are evenly coated.

Wrap in Foil:
- Carefully wrap the aluminum foil around the bananas, ensuring they are tightly sealed.

Cook Over the Campfire:
- Place the foil-wrapped bananas directly onto the hot coals of the campfire.
- Cook for about 5-10 minutes, flipping halfway through, or until the bananas are soft and caramelized.

Serve:
- Carefully unwrap the foil from the bananas and transfer them to serving plates.
- Optionally, serve with toppings such as chopped nuts, chocolate chips, whipped cream, or vanilla ice cream.

Campfire Caramelized Bananas are a sweet and indulgent treat that's quick and easy to make outdoors. Enjoy the warm, caramelized bananas straight from the campfire for a comforting and delicious dessert experience!

Dutch Oven Chocolate Chip Cookies

Ingredients:

- 2 cups all-purpose flour
- 1 teaspoon baking soda
- 1/2 teaspoon salt
- 3/4 cup unsalted butter, melted
- 1 cup packed brown sugar
- 1/2 cup granulated sugar
- 1 tablespoon vanilla extract
- 2 large eggs
- 1 1/2 cups semi-sweet chocolate chips

Instructions:

Prepare the Dutch Oven:
- Preheat your Dutch oven by placing it over the hot coals from your campfire.

Mix Dry Ingredients:
- In a large mixing bowl, whisk together the flour, baking soda, and salt.

Combine Wet Ingredients:
- In another bowl, mix together the melted butter, brown sugar, granulated sugar, and vanilla extract until well combined.
- Add the eggs one at a time, mixing well after each addition.

Combine Wet and Dry Ingredients:
- Gradually add the wet ingredients to the dry ingredients, stirring until just combined.
- Fold in the chocolate chips until evenly distributed throughout the dough.

Form Cookie Dough Balls:
- Scoop out portions of dough and roll them into balls, about 1-2 tablespoons of dough each.

Bake in the Dutch Oven:
- Place the cookie dough balls onto a parchment paper-lined Dutch oven, leaving space between each cookie for spreading.
- Cover the Dutch oven with its lid and place some hot coals on top of the lid.
- Bake for about 10-15 minutes, or until the cookies are golden brown around the edges. Rotate the Dutch oven occasionally for even cooking.

Cool and Serve:

- Once done, carefully remove the cookies from the Dutch oven and transfer them to a wire rack to cool completely.
- Enjoy your delicious Dutch Oven Chocolate Chip Cookies!

These Dutch Oven Chocolate Chip Cookies will be a hit with everyone around the campfire. They're warm, gooey, and full of chocolatey goodness, perfect for satisfying any sweet cravings during your outdoor adventures.

Campfire Rice Krispie Treats

Ingredients:

- 6 cups Rice Krispies cereal
- 1/4 cup unsalted butter
- 1 package (10 ounces) marshmallows
- Cooking spray or extra butter for greasing

Instructions:

Prepare the Campfire:
- Start by building a campfire and letting it burn down until you have hot coals.

Prepare the Marshmallow Mixture:
- In a large pot or Dutch oven, melt the butter over the campfire or on a camp stove.

Melt Marshmallows:
- Add the marshmallows to the melted butter and stir continuously until the marshmallows are completely melted and smooth.

Add Rice Krispies:
- Remove the pot from the heat source and stir in the Rice Krispies cereal until they are evenly coated with the melted marshmallow mixture.

Shape the Treats:
- Lightly grease a 9x13-inch baking dish or a square pan with cooking spray or butter.
- Transfer the Rice Krispie mixture into the greased baking dish.

Press Down Firmly:
- Use a spatula or wax paper to press down firmly on the mixture to create an even layer in the pan.

Let Them Cool:
- Allow the Rice Krispie treats to cool and set for about 30 minutes.

Cut Into Squares:
- Once cooled, cut the treats into squares using a sharp knife.

Enjoy:
- Serve the Campfire Rice Krispie Treats and enjoy them as a delicious snack or dessert around the campfire.

These Campfire Rice Krispie Treats are easy to make and perfect for satisfying your sweet tooth during outdoor adventures. They're gooey, crispy, and sure to be a hit with everyone!

Dutch Oven Mixed Berry Galette

Ingredients:

For the Galette Dough:

- 1 1/4 cups all-purpose flour
- 1/4 teaspoon salt
- 1 tablespoon granulated sugar
- 1/2 cup unsalted butter, cold and cut into cubes
- 3-4 tablespoons ice water

For the Filling:

- 3 cups mixed berries (such as strawberries, blueberries, raspberries, blackberries)
- 1/4 cup granulated sugar
- 2 tablespoons cornstarch
- Zest of 1 lemon
- 1 tablespoon lemon juice
- 1/2 teaspoon vanilla extract

For Assembly:

- 1 egg, beaten (for egg wash)
- Turbinado sugar, for sprinkling (optional)
- Whipped cream or vanilla ice cream, for serving (optional)

Instructions:

Prepare the Dutch Oven:
- Preheat your Dutch oven by placing it over hot coals to warm it up.

Make the Galette Dough:
- In a large bowl, whisk together the flour, salt, and granulated sugar.
- Add the cold cubed butter to the flour mixture and use a pastry cutter or your fingers to cut the butter into the flour until it resembles coarse crumbs.
- Slowly add the ice water, 1 tablespoon at a time, mixing with a fork until the dough just comes together. Be careful not to overwork the dough.
- Shape the dough into a disk, wrap it in plastic wrap, and chill it in a cooler or refrigerator while you prepare the filling.

Prepare the Filling:
- In a mixing bowl, combine the mixed berries, granulated sugar, cornstarch, lemon zest, lemon juice, and vanilla extract. Toss gently until the berries are coated evenly.

Roll Out the Dough:
- On a lightly floured surface, roll out the chilled dough into a rough circle about 1/8 inch thick.

Assemble the Galette:
- Carefully transfer the rolled-out dough to a piece of parchment paper.
- Arrange the mixed berry filling in the center of the dough, leaving about a 2-inch border around the edges.
- Fold the edges of the dough over the filling, pleating as you go, to create a rustic galette shape.

Bake in the Dutch Oven:
- Transfer the parchment paper with the assembled galette to the preheated Dutch oven.
- Brush the edges of the dough with the beaten egg and sprinkle with turbinado sugar, if desired.
- Cover the Dutch oven with its lid and place hot coals on top of the lid.
- Bake the galette for about 30-35 minutes, or until the crust is golden brown and the filling is bubbly.

Serve:
- Carefully remove the Dutch oven from the heat.
- Allow the galette to cool for a few minutes before slicing.
- Serve slices of the Dutch Oven Mixed Berry Galette warm, optionally topped with whipped cream or vanilla ice cream.

Enjoy the rustic charm and delicious flavors of this Dutch Oven Mixed Berry Galette, perfect for enjoying the bounty of summer while spending time outdoors.

Campfire Chocolate Fondue

Ingredients:

- 8 ounces semi-sweet chocolate, chopped
- 1/2 cup heavy cream
- 1 teaspoon vanilla extract
- Assorted dippers, such as:
    - Strawberries
    - Marshmallows
    - Pineapple chunks
    - Banana slices
    - Pretzel sticks
    - Pound cake cubes
    - Graham crackers

Instructions:

Prepare the Campfire:
- Start by building a campfire and letting it burn down until you have hot coals.

Make the Chocolate Fondue:
- In a heatproof bowl or pot, combine the chopped semi-sweet chocolate and heavy cream.
- Place the bowl or pot over the hot coals of the campfire, or use a camp stove if available.
- Stir the mixture continuously until the chocolate is melted and the mixture is smooth and creamy.

Add Vanilla Extract:
- Once the chocolate is melted, stir in the vanilla extract until well combined.

Serve:
- Transfer the melted chocolate fondue to a heatproof serving bowl or pot, placing it over a trivet or heatproof surface near the campfire.
- Arrange the assorted dippers on a platter or serving tray alongside the chocolate fondue.

Dip and Enjoy:
- Invite your guests to skewer their favorite dippers and dip them into the warm chocolate fondue.
- Enjoy the delicious combination of melted chocolate and various dippers around the campfire.

Campfire Chocolate Fondue is a fun and indulgent dessert that's sure to be a hit with everyone. It's perfect for sharing and adds a touch of sweetness to any outdoor gathering or camping adventure.

Dutch Oven Peach Dumplings

Ingredients:

For the Dumplings:

- 2 large ripe peaches, peeled and pitted
- 1 package (8 count) refrigerated crescent roll dough
- 1/2 cup unsalted butter
- 1 cup granulated sugar
- 1 teaspoon ground cinnamon
- 1/2 teaspoon vanilla extract

For Assembly:

- Ground cinnamon (for sprinkling)
- Vanilla ice cream or whipped cream (optional, for serving)

Instructions:

Prepare the Dutch Oven:
- Preheat your Dutch oven by placing it over hot coals to warm it up.

Prepare the Peaches:
- Cut each peeled and pitted peach into 4 wedges, yielding 8 total wedges.

Assemble the Dumplings:
- Unroll the crescent roll dough and separate it into 8 triangles.
- Place a peach wedge at the wide end of each triangle and roll it up, enclosing the peach inside the dough.

Make the Sauce:
- In a small saucepan or Dutch oven, melt the unsalted butter over the campfire.
- Stir in the granulated sugar, ground cinnamon, and vanilla extract until well combined and the sugar is dissolved, creating a sauce.

Arrange in the Dutch Oven:
- Place the peach dumplings in a single layer in the preheated Dutch oven.
- Pour the sauce evenly over the dumplings.

Bake in the Dutch Oven:
- Cover the Dutch oven with its lid and place hot coals on top of the lid.
- Bake for about 25-30 minutes, or until the dumplings are golden brown and cooked through.

Serve:

- Carefully remove the Dutch oven from the heat.
- Sprinkle the peach dumplings with ground cinnamon.
- Serve the Dutch Oven Peach Dumplings warm, optionally topped with a scoop of vanilla ice cream or whipped cream.

These Dutch Oven Peach Dumplings are a delightful and comforting dessert that's sure to impress your guests. Enjoy the warm, tender peaches wrapped in flaky dough, drizzled with a delicious cinnamon sugar sauce!

Camp Dutch Oven Berry Bread Pudding

Ingredients:

- 1 loaf of day-old bread (such as French bread), cut into cubes (about 8 cups)
- 2 cups mixed berries (such as raspberries, blueberries, blackberries)
- 4 large eggs
- 2 cups whole milk
- 1/2 cup heavy cream
- 1 cup granulated sugar
- 1 teaspoon vanilla extract
- 1/2 teaspoon ground cinnamon
- Pinch of salt
- Butter or cooking spray, for greasing the Dutch oven

Instructions:

Prepare the Dutch Oven:
- Grease the bottom and sides of a 10-inch Dutch oven with butter or cooking spray.

Prepare the Bread and Berries:
- Cut the day-old bread into cubes and spread them evenly in the prepared Dutch oven.
- Sprinkle the mixed berries over the bread cubes.

Make the Custard Mixture:
- In a large mixing bowl, whisk together the eggs, whole milk, heavy cream, granulated sugar, vanilla extract, ground cinnamon, and a pinch of salt until well combined.

Pour Custard Over Bread and Berries:
- Pour the custard mixture evenly over the bread cubes and mixed berries in the Dutch oven, making sure all the bread is soaked.

Let it Soak:
- Press down gently on the bread with a spatula or spoon to help the bread soak up the custard mixture.

Preheat the Dutch Oven:
- Place the Dutch oven over hot coals to preheat.

Bake:
- Once preheated, cover the Dutch oven with its lid and place hot coals on top of the lid.

- Bake for about 30-40 minutes, or until the bread pudding is set and golden brown on top. You can check for doneness by inserting a knife into the center – it should come out clean when the bread pudding is ready.

Serve:
- Carefully remove the Dutch oven from the heat and let the bread pudding cool for a few minutes.
- Serve warm and enjoy!

Camp Dutch Oven Berry Bread Pudding is a comforting and flavorful dessert that's perfect for sharing with friends and family around the campfire. The combination of juicy berries and custardy bread makes for a delightful treat in any outdoor setting.

Dutch Oven Key Lime Pie

Ingredients:

For the Crust:

- 1 1/2 cups graham cracker crumbs
- 1/4 cup granulated sugar
- 6 tablespoons unsalted butter, melted

For the Filling:

- 4 large egg yolks
- 1 can (14 ounces) sweetened condensed milk
- 1/2 cup freshly squeezed key lime juice
- Zest of 2 key limes (optional, for extra flavor)

For Topping (optional):

- Whipped cream
- Key lime slices or zest for garnish

Instructions:

Prepare the Dutch Oven:
- Preheat your Dutch oven by placing it over hot coals to warm it up.

Make the Crust:
- In a mixing bowl, combine the graham cracker crumbs, granulated sugar, and melted butter. Mix until well combined and the mixture resembles wet sand.

Press the Crust:
- Press the graham cracker mixture into the bottom and up the sides of a 9-inch pie dish or a Dutch oven, forming an even crust.

Make the Filling:
- In a separate mixing bowl, whisk together the egg yolks and sweetened condensed milk until smooth.
- Gradually add the key lime juice and zest (if using), whisking until well combined.

Pour the Filling:
- Pour the key lime filling into the prepared crust, spreading it out evenly.

Bake in the Dutch Oven:

- Place the pie dish or Dutch oven with the key lime pie filling into the preheated Dutch oven.
- Cover the Dutch oven with its lid and place hot coals on top of the lid.
- Bake for about 20-25 minutes, or until the filling is set and the edges are lightly golden brown.

Chill:
- Once done, remove the Dutch oven from the heat and let the key lime pie cool to room temperature.
- Refrigerate the pie for at least 2 hours, or until chilled and set.

Serve:
- Optionally, garnish the chilled key lime pie with whipped cream and key lime slices or zest.
- Slice and serve the Dutch Oven Key Lime Pie, and enjoy its refreshing citrus flavor!

This Dutch Oven Key Lime Pie is a refreshing and tangy dessert that's perfect for enjoying outdoors. Its creamy filling and buttery graham cracker crust make it a delightful treat for any outdoor gathering or camping adventure.

Campfire Grilled Peaches

Ingredients:

- Ripe peaches, halved and pitted
- Honey or maple syrup (optional)
- Cinnamon (optional)
- Vanilla ice cream or whipped cream (optional, for serving)

Instructions:

Prepare the Campfire:
- Start by building a campfire and letting it burn down until you have hot coals.

Prepare the Peaches:
- Cut the peaches in half and remove the pits. Leave the skins on for grilling.

Grill the Peaches:
- Place the peach halves directly on the grill grate, cut side down.

Grill Until Tender:
- Grill the peaches for about 3-5 minutes on each side, or until they are tender and have grill marks.

Optional Sweetening:
- If desired, drizzle honey or maple syrup over the grilled peaches for added sweetness. Sprinkle with a little cinnamon for extra flavor.

Serve:
- Serve the grilled peaches warm.
- Optionally, top each peach half with a scoop of vanilla ice cream or a dollop of whipped cream for a delicious dessert.

Campfire grilled peaches are a simple yet elegant dessert that's perfect for outdoor gatherings. They're easy to make and bursting with flavor, making them a delightful treat for any camping trip or cookout. Enjoy the warm and caramelized peaches straight from the grill!

Dutch Oven Cranberry Orange Bread

Ingredients:

- 2 cups all-purpose flour
- 1 cup granulated sugar
- 1 teaspoon baking powder
- 1/2 teaspoon baking soda
- 1/2 teaspoon salt
- Zest of 1 orange
- 3/4 cup orange juice
- 1/4 cup unsalted butter, melted
- 1 large egg
- 1 teaspoon vanilla extract
- 1 cup fresh cranberries, chopped
- Optional: additional orange zest and sugar for topping

Instructions:

Prepare the Dutch Oven:
- Preheat your Dutch oven by placing it over hot coals to warm it up.

Mix Dry Ingredients:
- In a large mixing bowl, whisk together the flour, sugar, baking powder, baking soda, salt, and orange zest.

Combine Wet Ingredients:
- In a separate bowl, whisk together the orange juice, melted butter, egg, and vanilla extract until well combined.

Combine Wet and Dry Ingredients:
- Gradually add the wet ingredients to the dry ingredients, stirring until just combined. Be careful not to overmix.
- Fold in the chopped cranberries until evenly distributed throughout the batter.

Transfer to Dutch Oven:
- Grease the bottom and sides of the preheated Dutch oven with butter or cooking spray.
- Pour the batter into the Dutch oven, spreading it out evenly.

Bake in Dutch Oven:
- Cover the Dutch oven with its lid and place hot coals on top of the lid.
- Bake for about 45-55 minutes, or until the bread is golden brown and a toothpick inserted into the center comes out clean.

Optional Topping:
- If desired, sprinkle additional orange zest and sugar over the top of the bread during the last 10-15 minutes of baking for added flavor and decoration.

Cool and Serve:
- Once done, carefully remove the Dutch oven from the heat.
- Allow the bread to cool in the Dutch oven for a few minutes before transferring it to a wire rack to cool completely.
- Slice and serve the Dutch Oven Cranberry Orange Bread, and enjoy its delicious flavor!

This Dutch Oven Cranberry Orange Bread is moist, flavorful, and perfect for enjoying as a snack or dessert during outdoor adventures. The combination of tart cranberries and zesty orange makes it a delightful treat for any occasion.

Camp Dutch Oven Tiramisu

Ingredients:

- 1 pound mascarpone cheese
- 1 cup heavy cream
- 1/2 cup granulated sugar
- 1 teaspoon vanilla extract
- 1/4 cup brewed coffee or espresso, cooled
- 2 tablespoons coffee liqueur (optional)
- Ladyfinger cookies (Savoiardi)
- Cocoa powder, for dusting

Instructions:

Prepare the Dutch Oven:
- Preheat your camp Dutch oven by placing it over hot coals to warm it up.

Make the Mascarpone Mixture:
- In a large mixing bowl, beat together the mascarpone cheese, heavy cream, granulated sugar, and vanilla extract until smooth and creamy. Set aside.

Prepare the Coffee Mixture:
- In a shallow dish, combine the cooled brewed coffee or espresso with the coffee liqueur (if using).

Assemble the Tiramisu:
- Dip each ladyfinger cookie into the coffee mixture briefly, ensuring they are evenly soaked but not overly soggy.
- Arrange a layer of soaked ladyfinger cookies in the bottom of the preheated Dutch oven.

Add Mascarpone Layer:
- Spread half of the mascarpone mixture over the layer of ladyfinger cookies in the Dutch oven, smoothing it out evenly.

Repeat Layers:
- Repeat the process with another layer of soaked ladyfinger cookies followed by the remaining mascarpone mixture.

Dust with Cocoa Powder:
- Dust the top of the Tiramisu with cocoa powder using a fine-mesh sieve, covering it evenly.

Bake in Dutch Oven:
- Cover the Dutch oven with its lid and place hot coals on top of the lid.

- Bake the Tiramisu in the Dutch oven for about 30-40 minutes, or until the top is set and the edges are golden brown.

Serve:
- Carefully remove the Dutch oven from the heat and let the Tiramisu cool slightly.
- Serve the Camp Dutch Oven Tiramisu warm, scooping out portions directly from the Dutch oven.

This Camp Dutch Oven Tiramisu offers a warm and comforting twist on the classic dessert, perfect for enjoying around the campfire with friends and family. The creamy mascarpone cheese, coffee-soaked ladyfingers, and dusting of cocoa powder create a delicious treat that's sure to impress.

Dutch Oven Apricot Crisp

Ingredients:

For the Filling:

- 6 cups fresh apricots, pitted and sliced
- 1/2 cup granulated sugar
- 2 tablespoons all-purpose flour
- 1 teaspoon vanilla extract
- 1/2 teaspoon ground cinnamon

For the Crisp Topping:

- 1 cup old-fashioned rolled oats
- 1/2 cup all-purpose flour
- 1/2 cup brown sugar
- 1/2 teaspoon ground cinnamon
- 1/4 teaspoon salt
- 1/2 cup unsalted butter, cold and cubed

Instructions:

Prepare the Dutch Oven:
- Preheat your Dutch oven by placing it over hot coals to warm it up.

Make the Apricot Filling:
- In a large mixing bowl, combine the sliced apricots, granulated sugar, all-purpose flour, vanilla extract, and ground cinnamon. Toss until the apricots are evenly coated.

Prepare the Crisp Topping:
- In another mixing bowl, combine the rolled oats, all-purpose flour, brown sugar, ground cinnamon, and salt.
- Add the cold cubed butter to the mixture and use your fingers or a pastry cutter to cut the butter into the dry ingredients until it resembles coarse crumbs.

Assemble the Crisp:
- Spread the prepared apricot filling evenly in the preheated Dutch oven.

Add the Crisp Topping:
- Sprinkle the crisp topping mixture evenly over the apricot filling in the Dutch oven, covering it completely.

Bake in Dutch Oven:

- Cover the Dutch oven with its lid and place hot coals on top of the lid.
- Bake the apricot crisp in the Dutch oven for about 30-40 minutes, or until the filling is bubbly and the topping is golden brown and crispy.

Serve:
- Carefully remove the Dutch oven from the heat.
- Let the apricot crisp cool slightly before serving.
- Serve warm, optionally topped with a scoop of vanilla ice cream or a dollop of whipped cream.

This Dutch Oven Apricot Crisp is a delightful and comforting dessert that's perfect for enjoying outdoors. The combination of sweet apricots and crispy oat topping makes it a satisfying treat for any camping adventure or outdoor gathering.

Campfire Cinnamon Sugar Donuts

Ingredients:

- 1 can (16.3 ounces) refrigerated biscuit dough (such as Grands!®)
- Vegetable oil for frying
- 1/2 cup granulated sugar
- 1 tablespoon ground cinnamon

Instructions:

Prepare the Campfire:
- Start by building a campfire and letting it burn down until you have hot coals.

Prepare the Donuts:
- Open the can of refrigerated biscuit dough and separate the biscuits.
- Use your thumb or a small round cutter to create a hole in the center of each biscuit, forming a donut shape. You can use the removed dough to make donut holes.

Fry the Donuts:
- In a Dutch oven or large pot, heat vegetable oil over the campfire until it reaches about 350°F (175°C).
- Carefully add the donuts to the hot oil, a few at a time, making sure not to overcrowd the pot.
- Fry the donuts for about 1-2 minutes on each side, or until they are golden brown and cooked through.
- Use a slotted spoon or tongs to remove the donuts from the oil and transfer them to a plate lined with paper towels to drain excess oil.

Coat with Cinnamon Sugar:
- In a shallow bowl, mix together the granulated sugar and ground cinnamon until well combined.
- While the donuts are still warm, roll them in the cinnamon sugar mixture, coating them evenly on all sides.

Serve:
- Serve the Campfire Cinnamon Sugar Donuts warm and enjoy them as a delicious outdoor treat.

These Campfire Cinnamon Sugar Donuts are crispy on the outside, fluffy on the inside, and coated with a sweet and fragrant cinnamon sugar mixture. They're perfect for enjoying around the campfire with friends and family!

Dutch Oven Coconut Macaroons

Ingredients:

- 3 cups sweetened shredded coconut
- 3/4 cup sweetened condensed milk
- 2 large egg whites
- 1 teaspoon vanilla extract
- Pinch of salt

Instructions:

Prepare the Dutch Oven:
- Preheat your Dutch oven by placing it over hot coals to warm it up.

Mix Ingredients:
- In a large mixing bowl, combine the sweetened shredded coconut, sweetened condensed milk, vanilla extract, and a pinch of salt. Mix until well combined.

Whip Egg Whites:
- In a separate bowl, beat the egg whites until stiff peaks form.

Fold in Egg Whites:
- Gently fold the beaten egg whites into the coconut mixture until evenly incorporated.

Form Macaroons:
- Using a spoon or cookie scoop, scoop out portions of the coconut mixture and shape them into small mounds, placing them on a parchment paper-lined surface.

Bake in Dutch Oven:
- Place the parchment paper with the shaped macaroons into the preheated Dutch oven.
- Cover the Dutch oven with its lid and place hot coals on top of the lid.
- Bake for about 15-20 minutes, or until the macaroons are lightly golden brown on the outside and set.

Cool and Serve:
- Once done, carefully remove the Dutch oven from the heat.
- Let the macaroons cool on the parchment paper for a few minutes before transferring them to a wire rack to cool completely.

Serve:
- Serve the Dutch Oven Coconut Macaroons once cooled, and enjoy their sweet and chewy coconut flavor!

These Dutch Oven Coconut Macaroons are a simple yet delicious treat that's perfect for enjoying around the campfire. They're sweet, chewy, and packed with coconut flavor, making them a delightful dessert for outdoor adventures.

Camp Dutch Oven Berry Cobbler Bars

Ingredients:

For the Berry Filling:

- 4 cups mixed berries (such as strawberries, blueberries, raspberries, blackberries)
- 1/2 cup granulated sugar
- 2 tablespoons cornstarch
- 1 tablespoon lemon juice
- Zest of 1 lemon (optional, for extra flavor)

For the Cobbler Crust and Topping:

- 1 1/2 cups all-purpose flour
- 1 cup old-fashioned oats
- 3/4 cup granulated sugar
- 1/2 teaspoon baking powder
- 1/4 teaspoon salt
- 1 cup unsalted butter, melted
- 1 teaspoon vanilla extract

Instructions:

Prepare the Campfire:
- Start by building a campfire and letting it burn down until you have hot coals.

Prepare the Berry Filling:
- In a large bowl, combine the mixed berries, granulated sugar, cornstarch, lemon juice, and lemon zest (if using). Toss until the berries are coated evenly. Set aside.

Make the Cobbler Crust and Topping:
- In another large bowl, mix together the all-purpose flour, old-fashioned oats, granulated sugar, baking powder, and salt.
- Stir in the melted butter and vanilla extract until the mixture resembles coarse crumbs.

Assemble the Cobbler:
- Grease the bottom and sides of a 12-inch camp Dutch oven with butter or cooking spray.

- Spread half of the cobbler crust and topping mixture into the bottom of the Dutch oven, pressing down gently to form an even layer.
- Spread the berry filling over the crust layer in the Dutch oven.
- Sprinkle the remaining cobbler crust and topping mixture evenly over the berry filling.

Bake in Dutch Oven:
- Cover the Dutch oven with its lid and place hot coals on top of the lid.
- Bake the berry cobbler bars in the Dutch oven for about 35-45 minutes, or until the crust is golden brown and the berry filling is bubbly.

Cool and Serve:
- Once done, carefully remove the Dutch oven from the heat.
- Let the berry cobbler bars cool slightly before slicing and serving.

These Camp Dutch Oven Berry Cobbler Bars are a delicious and comforting dessert that's perfect for sharing with friends and family around the campfire. Enjoy the sweet and tangy flavors of the mixed berries paired with the buttery oat crust!

Dutch Oven Lemon Poppy Seed Cake

Ingredients:

- 1 1/2 cups all-purpose flour
- 1/2 teaspoon baking powder
- 1/4 teaspoon baking soda
- 1/4 teaspoon salt
- Zest of 1 lemon
- 1 tablespoon poppy seeds
- 1/2 cup unsalted butter, softened
- 1 cup granulated sugar
- 2 large eggs
- 1/4 cup freshly squeezed lemon juice
- 1/2 cup buttermilk
- Powdered sugar, for dusting (optional)

Instructions:

Prepare the Dutch Oven:
- Preheat your Dutch oven by placing it over hot coals to warm it up.

Mix Dry Ingredients:
- In a medium bowl, whisk together the all-purpose flour, baking powder, baking soda, salt, lemon zest, and poppy seeds. Set aside.

Cream Butter and Sugar:
- In a large mixing bowl, cream together the softened unsalted butter and granulated sugar until light and fluffy.

Add Eggs and Lemon Juice:
- Beat in the eggs, one at a time, until well combined.
- Mix in the freshly squeezed lemon juice until incorporated.

Alternate Adding Dry Ingredients and Buttermilk:
- Gradually add the dry ingredients mixture to the wet ingredients, alternating with the buttermilk. Begin and end with the dry ingredients, mixing until just combined after each addition. Be careful not to overmix.

Transfer Batter to Dutch Oven:
- Grease the bottom and sides of the preheated Dutch oven with butter or cooking spray.
- Pour the batter into the Dutch oven, spreading it out evenly.

Bake in Dutch Oven:
- Cover the Dutch oven with its lid and place hot coals on top of the lid.

- Bake the lemon poppy seed cake in the Dutch oven for about 30-40 minutes, or until a toothpick inserted into the center comes out clean.

Cool and Serve:
- Once done, carefully remove the Dutch oven from the heat.
- Let the cake cool in the Dutch oven for a few minutes before transferring it to a wire rack to cool completely.
- Dust the cooled lemon poppy seed cake with powdered sugar, if desired.

This Dutch Oven Lemon Poppy Seed Cake is moist, flavorful, and bursting with citrusy goodness. It's a perfect dessert to enjoy outdoors with friends and family!

Campfire Apple Cider Doughnuts

Ingredients:

- 2 cups apple cider
- 2 cups all-purpose flour
- 1 1/2 teaspoons baking powder
- 1/2 teaspoon baking soda
- 1 teaspoon ground cinnamon
- 1/4 teaspoon ground nutmeg
- 1/4 teaspoon salt
- 1/2 cup granulated sugar
- 1/4 cup unsalted butter, melted
- 1 large egg
- 1 teaspoon vanilla extract
- Vegetable oil, for frying
- Cinnamon sugar (optional, for coating)

Instructions:

Reduce Apple Cider:
- In a small saucepan, simmer the apple cider over medium heat until it reduces to about 1/2 cup, stirring occasionally. This process may take about 15-20 minutes. Remove from heat and let it cool.

Prepare Dry Ingredients:
- In a mixing bowl, whisk together the all-purpose flour, baking powder, baking soda, ground cinnamon, ground nutmeg, and salt. Set aside.

Mix Wet Ingredients:
- In another mixing bowl, whisk together the reduced apple cider, granulated sugar, melted unsalted butter, egg, and vanilla extract until well combined.

Combine Wet and Dry Ingredients:
- Gradually add the dry ingredients to the wet ingredients, stirring until just combined. Be careful not to overmix.

Chill Dough:
- Cover the dough and chill it in the refrigerator for about 1 hour to make it easier to handle.

Shape Doughnuts:
- After chilling, roll out the dough on a floured surface to about 1/2-inch thickness.

- Use a doughnut cutter or two round cutters (one larger for the outer circle and one smaller for the inner circle) to cut out doughnuts and doughnut holes.

Fry Doughnuts:
- In a Dutch oven or deep frying pan, heat vegetable oil to 350°F (175°C).
- Carefully add the doughnuts to the hot oil, a few at a time, and fry until golden brown on both sides, about 1-2 minutes per side.
- Use a slotted spoon to transfer the fried doughnuts to a plate lined with paper towels to drain excess oil.

Coat with Cinnamon Sugar:
- While still warm, roll the fried doughnuts in cinnamon sugar to coat them evenly, if desired.

Serve:
- Serve the Campfire Apple Cider Doughnuts warm and enjoy them as a delicious treat around the campfire.

These Campfire Apple Cider Doughnuts are fluffy, flavorful, and infused with the taste of apple cider and warm spices. They're sure to be a hit with everyone gathered around the campfire!

Dutch Oven Rhubarb Crisp

Ingredients:

For the Filling:

- 4 cups chopped rhubarb (about 1-inch pieces)
- 1 cup granulated sugar
- 2 tablespoons all-purpose flour
- 1 teaspoon vanilla extract

For the Crisp Topping:

- 1 cup old-fashioned rolled oats
- 1/2 cup all-purpose flour
- 1/2 cup packed brown sugar
- 1/2 teaspoon ground cinnamon
- 1/4 teaspoon salt
- 1/2 cup unsalted butter, melted

Instructions:

Prepare the Dutch Oven:
- Preheat your Dutch oven by placing it over hot coals to warm it up.

Make the Rhubarb Filling:
- In a large mixing bowl, combine the chopped rhubarb, granulated sugar, all-purpose flour, and vanilla extract. Toss until the rhubarb is evenly coated.

Transfer to Dutch Oven:
- Grease the bottom and sides of the preheated Dutch oven with butter or cooking spray.
- Pour the rhubarb mixture into the Dutch oven, spreading it out evenly.

Make the Crisp Topping:
- In a separate mixing bowl, combine the rolled oats, all-purpose flour, brown sugar, ground cinnamon, and salt.
- Pour the melted unsalted butter over the dry ingredients and mix until the mixture resembles coarse crumbs.

Top the Rhubarb with Crisp Topping:
- Sprinkle the crisp topping evenly over the rhubarb filling in the Dutch oven.

Bake in Dutch Oven:
- Cover the Dutch oven with its lid and place hot coals on top of the lid.

- Bake the rhubarb crisp in the Dutch oven for about 30-40 minutes, or until the rhubarb is tender and the topping is golden brown and crispy.

Serve:
- Carefully remove the Dutch oven from the heat.
- Let the rhubarb crisp cool slightly before serving.
- Serve the Dutch Oven Rhubarb Crisp warm, optionally topped with vanilla ice cream or whipped cream.

This Dutch Oven Rhubarb Crisp is a delightful dessert that perfectly balances the tartness of rhubarb with the sweetness of the crisp topping. Enjoy it as a comforting treat during outdoor gatherings or camping trips!

Camp Dutch Oven Almond Joy Brownies

Ingredients:

For the Brownie Batter:

- 1 cup (2 sticks) unsalted butter
- 2 cups granulated sugar
- 4 large eggs
- 1 teaspoon vanilla extract
- 1 cup all-purpose flour
- 3/4 cup unsweetened cocoa powder
- 1/2 teaspoon salt

For the Topping:

- 1 cup sweetened shredded coconut
- 1/2 cup sliced almonds
- 1 cup semisweet chocolate chips
- 1/2 cup sweetened condensed milk

Instructions:

Prepare the Dutch Oven:
- Preheat your camp Dutch oven by placing it over hot coals to warm it up.

Make the Brownie Batter:
- In a small saucepan or over a camp stove, melt the unsalted butter.
- In a large mixing bowl, combine the melted butter with granulated sugar, eggs, and vanilla extract. Mix until well combined.
- Stir in the all-purpose flour, unsweetened cocoa powder, and salt until just combined, being careful not to overmix.

Pour Batter into Dutch Oven:
- Grease the bottom and sides of the preheated Dutch oven with butter or cooking spray.
- Pour the brownie batter into the Dutch oven, spreading it out evenly.

Prepare the Topping:
- In a small bowl, mix together the sweetened shredded coconut and sliced almonds.
- Sprinkle the coconut and almond mixture evenly over the brownie batter in the Dutch oven.

Add Chocolate Layer:

- Sprinkle the semisweet chocolate chips evenly over the coconut and almond mixture.
- Drizzle the sweetened condensed milk over the chocolate chips.

Bake in Dutch Oven:
- Cover the Dutch oven with its lid and place hot coals on top of the lid.
- Bake the brownies in the Dutch oven for about 30-35 minutes, or until the edges are set and the top is slightly firm.

Cool and Serve:
- Carefully remove the Dutch oven from the heat.
- Let the brownies cool in the Dutch oven for a few minutes before slicing and serving.

These Camp Dutch Oven Almond Joy Brownies are rich, chocolaty, and loaded with the flavors of almonds and coconut. They're perfect for satisfying your sweet tooth during outdoor adventures!

Dutch Oven Cherry Chocolate Cake

Ingredients:

- 1 box (15.25 ounces) chocolate cake mix
- 1 can (21 ounces) cherry pie filling
- 3 large eggs
- 1 teaspoon almond extract (optional)
- 1/2 cup semisweet chocolate chips
- Cooking spray or butter, for greasing the Dutch oven

Instructions:

Prepare the Dutch Oven:
- Preheat your Dutch oven by placing it over hot coals to warm it up.

Mix Cake Batter:
- In a large mixing bowl, combine the chocolate cake mix, cherry pie filling, eggs, and almond extract (if using). Mix until well combined and smooth.

Add Chocolate Chips:
- Fold in the semisweet chocolate chips until evenly distributed throughout the batter.

Grease Dutch Oven:
- Grease the bottom and sides of the preheated Dutch oven with cooking spray or butter.

Pour Batter into Dutch Oven:
- Pour the cake batter into the greased Dutch oven, spreading it out evenly.

Bake in Dutch Oven:
- Cover the Dutch oven with its lid and place hot coals on top of the lid.
- Bake the cake in the Dutch oven for about 35-45 minutes, or until a toothpick inserted into the center comes out clean.

Cool and Serve:
- Carefully remove the Dutch oven from the heat.
- Let the cake cool in the Dutch oven for a few minutes before slicing and serving.

This Dutch Oven Cherry Chocolate Cake is moist, flavorful, and bursting with the combination of chocolate and cherries. It's a perfect dessert to enjoy during outdoor gatherings or camping trips!

Campfire Caramel Apple Nachos

Ingredients:

- 2-3 large apples, cored and thinly sliced (use varieties like Granny Smith or Honeycrisp)
- Caramel sauce (homemade or store-bought)
- Chocolate sauce or melted chocolate chips
- Chopped nuts (such as peanuts, almonds, or pecans), optional
- Mini marshmallows, optional
- Crushed graham crackers or cinnamon sugar, optional

Instructions:

Prepare the Apples:
- Core the apples and thinly slice them into rounds. You can leave the peel on or remove it according to your preference. Arrange the apple slices on a serving platter or a heatproof tray.

Drizzle with Caramel Sauce:
- Drizzle the sliced apples generously with caramel sauce. You can use store-bought caramel sauce or make your own by melting caramel candies with a bit of cream.

Add Chocolate Sauce:
- Drizzle chocolate sauce over the caramel-covered apples. Alternatively, melt chocolate chips in the microwave or over a campfire and drizzle the melted chocolate over the apples.

Optional Toppings:
- Sprinkle chopped nuts, such as peanuts, almonds, or pecans, over the caramel and chocolate-covered apples for added crunch and flavor.
- Scatter mini marshmallows over the top for a gooey, campfire-inspired touch.
- Sprinkle crushed graham crackers or cinnamon sugar over the nachos for an extra layer of sweetness and texture.

Warm Over Campfire:
- Place the tray of caramel apple nachos over a campfire, using a wire rack or a grill grate if available. Alternatively, you can use a portable camping stove or grill.
- Heat the nachos over the campfire until the toppings are warmed and gooey, and the apples are slightly softened. Be careful not to burn the toppings.

Serve Warm:
- Once warmed, carefully remove the tray of caramel apple nachos from the campfire.
- Serve the nachos immediately while warm, allowing everyone to dig in and enjoy the delicious combination of flavors.

Campfire Caramel Apple Nachos are a fun and easy-to-make dessert that's perfect for enjoying around the campfire with friends and family. They're customizable with various toppings and are sure to be a hit at any outdoor gathering or camping trip!

Dutch Oven Butterscotch Pudding

Ingredients:

- 1/2 cup (1 stick) unsalted butter
- 1 cup packed brown sugar
- 1/4 cup cornstarch
- 1/2 teaspoon salt
- 4 cups whole milk
- 4 large egg yolks
- 2 teaspoons vanilla extract

Instructions:

Prepare the Dutch Oven:
- Preheat your Dutch oven by placing it over hot coals to warm it up.

Melt Butter and Brown Sugar:
- In the preheated Dutch oven, melt the unsalted butter over medium heat.
- Add the packed brown sugar to the melted butter and stir until the sugar is dissolved and the mixture is smooth.

Mix Cornstarch and Salt:
- In a separate bowl, whisk together the cornstarch and salt until well combined.

Add Milk:
- Gradually pour the whole milk into the Dutch oven with the melted butter and brown sugar mixture, stirring continuously.

Add Cornstarch Mixture:
- Gradually whisk the cornstarch mixture into the milk mixture in the Dutch oven, stirring constantly to prevent lumps from forming.

Cook Until Thickened:
- Continue cooking the pudding mixture over medium heat, stirring constantly, until it thickens and comes to a gentle boil. This may take about 5-7 minutes.

Temper Egg Yolks:
- In a separate bowl, whisk the egg yolks until smooth.
- Gradually add a small amount of the hot pudding mixture to the egg yolks while whisking constantly. This process helps to temper the egg yolks and prevent them from curdling when added to the hot pudding.

Add Egg Yolks to Pudding:

- Pour the tempered egg yolk mixture back into the Dutch oven with the pudding mixture, stirring continuously.

Cook Until Thickened:
- Cook the pudding mixture for an additional 2-3 minutes, stirring constantly, until it thickens further.

Remove from Heat and Add Vanilla:
- Remove the Dutch oven from the heat.
- Stir in the vanilla extract until well combined.

Serve Warm or Chill:
- Serve the Dutch Oven Butterscotch Pudding warm directly from the Dutch oven or transfer it to individual serving dishes.
- Alternatively, you can chill the pudding in the refrigerator for a few hours until it's cold and set before serving.

This Dutch Oven Butterscotch Pudding is rich, creamy, and full of comforting flavors.

Enjoy it as a delightful dessert during your outdoor adventures!

Camp Dutch Oven Peanut Butter Cup S'mores

Ingredients:

- Graham crackers
- Peanut butter cups (such as Reese's)
- Marshmallows

Instructions:

Prepare the Dutch Oven:
- Preheat your camp Dutch oven by placing it over hot coals to warm it up.

Assemble the S'mores:
- Break the graham crackers in half to form squares.
- Place a square of graham cracker on a heatproof surface.
- Top the graham cracker square with a peanut butter cup.

Add Marshmallows:
- Place a marshmallow on top of the peanut butter cup.

Close S'mores:
- Place another square of graham cracker on top of the marshmallow to form a sandwich.

Wrap in Foil (Optional):
- If desired, wrap each assembled s'more in aluminum foil to help contain the ingredients while they heat up.

Heat in Dutch Oven:
- Carefully place the wrapped or unwrapped s'mores in the preheated Dutch oven.

Cook Until Marshmallows are Gooey:
- Cook the s'mores in the Dutch oven for a few minutes, until the marshmallows are gooey and the peanut butter cups are slightly melted.

Serve Warm:
- Carefully remove the s'mores from the Dutch oven.
- Unwrap if they were wrapped in foil.
- Serve the Camp Dutch Oven Peanut Butter Cup S'mores warm and enjoy the gooey, chocolatey, peanut buttery goodness!

These Camp Dutch Oven Peanut Butter Cup S'mores are sure to be a hit around the campfire. They're quick and easy to make, and the combination of peanut butter cups with marshmallows and graham crackers is irresistible. Enjoy them during your outdoor adventures!

Dutch Oven Raspberry Cheesecake

Ingredients:

For the Crust:

- 1 1/2 cups graham cracker crumbs
- 1/4 cup granulated sugar
- 1/2 cup unsalted butter, melted

For the Cheesecake Filling:

- 24 ounces cream cheese, softened
- 1 cup granulated sugar
- 3 large eggs
- 1 teaspoon vanilla extract
- 1/4 cup sour cream

For the Raspberry Swirl:

- 1 cup fresh or frozen raspberries
- 2 tablespoons granulated sugar
- 1 tablespoon lemon juice
- 1 tablespoon water
- 1 tablespoon cornstarch

Instructions:

Prepare the Dutch Oven:
- Preheat your camp Dutch oven by placing it over hot coals to warm it up.

Make the Crust:
- In a mixing bowl, combine the graham cracker crumbs, granulated sugar, and melted unsalted butter. Mix until well combined.
- Press the mixture firmly into the bottom of the preheated Dutch oven to form the crust.

Make the Cheesecake Filling:
- In a large mixing bowl, beat the softened cream cheese and granulated sugar until smooth.
- Add the eggs, one at a time, beating well after each addition.
- Stir in the vanilla extract and sour cream until well combined.

Prepare the Raspberry Swirl:

- In a small saucepan, combine the raspberries, granulated sugar, lemon juice, water, and cornstarch.
- Cook over medium heat, stirring constantly, until the mixture thickens and the raspberries break down, about 5-7 minutes. Remove from heat and let it cool slightly.

Assemble the Cheesecake:
- Pour the cheesecake filling over the graham cracker crust in the Dutch oven, spreading it out evenly.
- Spoon dollops of the raspberry swirl mixture over the cheesecake filling.
- Use a knife to gently swirl the raspberry mixture into the cheesecake filling, creating a marbled effect.

Bake in Dutch Oven:
- Cover the Dutch oven with its lid and place hot coals on top of the lid.
- Bake the cheesecake in the Dutch oven for about 45-55 minutes, or until the edges are set and the center is slightly jiggly.

Cool and Chill:
- Once done, carefully remove the Dutch oven from the heat.
- Let the cheesecake cool in the Dutch oven for about 1 hour, then transfer it to a cooler place to cool completely.
- Chill the cheesecake in the refrigerator for at least 4 hours or overnight before serving.

Serve:
- Once chilled, slice the Dutch Oven Raspberry Cheesecake into portions and serve. Enjoy the creamy cheesecake with swirls of raspberry goodness!

This Dutch Oven Raspberry Cheesecake is a decadent and flavorful dessert that's perfect for outdoor gatherings or camping trips. The creamy cheesecake paired with the tangy raspberry swirls creates a delightful treat for any occasion.

Campfire Trail Mix Bars

Ingredients:

- 2 cups old-fashioned rolled oats
- 1 cup crispy rice cereal
- 1/2 cup chopped nuts (such as almonds, pecans, or walnuts)
- 1/2 cup dried fruits (such as raisins, cranberries, or chopped apricots)
- 1/2 cup chocolate chips or chunks
- 1/2 cup honey
- 1/4 cup peanut butter or almond butter
- 1/4 cup brown sugar
- 1 teaspoon vanilla extract
- 1/4 teaspoon salt

Instructions:

Prepare the Campfire:
- If you're making these bars at a campsite, prepare your campfire or portable stove for cooking.

Mix Dry Ingredients:
- In a large mixing bowl, combine the old-fashioned rolled oats, crispy rice cereal, chopped nuts, dried fruits, and chocolate chips. Stir to mix well.

Prepare the Binding Mixture:
- In a small saucepan, combine the honey, peanut butter (or almond butter), brown sugar, vanilla extract, and salt.
- Heat the mixture over medium heat, stirring constantly, until the ingredients are well combined and the mixture is smooth. This should take about 3-4 minutes.

Combine Wet and Dry Ingredients:
- Pour the hot binding mixture over the dry ingredients in the mixing bowl.
- Stir well until all the dry ingredients are evenly coated with the binding mixture.

Press into Pan:
- Line a 9x9-inch baking dish with parchment paper or aluminum foil, leaving some overhang on the sides for easy removal.
- Transfer the mixture into the prepared baking dish.
- Use a spatula or the back of a spoon to press the mixture firmly and evenly into the pan.

Chill and Set:

- Place the baking dish in the refrigerator for at least 1 hour to allow the bars to chill and set.

Slice into Bars:
- Once chilled and set, remove the baking dish from the refrigerator.
- Use the overhanging parchment paper or aluminum foil to lift the bars out of the pan.
- Place them on a cutting board and slice into individual bars using a sharp knife.

Serve and Enjoy:
- Serve the Campfire Trail Mix Bars immediately, or store them in an airtight container for later enjoyment.
- These bars are perfect for snacking on the go during outdoor activities or camping trips.

These Campfire Trail Mix Bars are versatile, customizable, and packed with delicious flavors and textures. Enjoy them as a tasty and energizing snack during your outdoor adventures!